Worldwide Threat Assessment
of the
US Intelligence Community

February 26, 2015

WORLDWIDE THREAT ASSESSMENT
of the
US INTELLIGENCE COMMUNITY

February 26, 2015

INTRODUCTION

Chairman McCain, Ranking Member Reed, Members of the Committee, thank you for the invitation to offer the United States Intelligence Community's 2015 assessment of threats to US national security. My statement reflects the collective insights of the Intelligence Community's extraordinary men and women, whom I am privileged and honored to lead. We in the Intelligence Community are committed every day to provide the nuanced, multidisciplinary intelligence that policymakers, warfighters, and domestic law enforcement personnel need to protect American lives and America's interests anywhere in the world.

Information available as of February 13, 2015 was used in the preparation of this assessment.

TABLE OF CONTENTS

GLOBAL THREATS

REGIONAL THREATS

GLOBAL THREATS

CYBER

Strategic Assessment

Cyber threats to US national and economic security are increasing in frequency, scale, sophistication, and severity of impact. The ranges of cyber threat actors, methods of attack, targeted systems, and victims are also expanding. Overall, the unclassified information and communication technology (ICT) networks that support US Government, military, commercial, and social activities remain vulnerable to espionage and/or disruption. However, the likelihood of a catastrophic attack from any particular actor is remote at this time. Rather than a "Cyber Armageddon" scenario that debilitates the entire US infrastructure, we envision something different. We foresee an ongoing series of low-to-moderate level cyber attacks from a variety of sources over time, which will impose cumulative costs on US economic competitiveness and national security.

- A growing number of computer forensic studies by industry experts strongly suggest that several nations—including Iran and North Korea—have undertaken offensive cyber operations against private sector targets to support their economic and foreign policy objectives, at times concurrent with political crises.

Risk. Despite ever-improving network defenses, the diverse possibilities for remote hacking intrusions, supply chain operations to insert compromised hardware or software, and malevolent activities by human insiders will hold nearly all ICT systems at risk for years to come. In short, the cyber threat cannot be eliminated; rather, cyber risk must be managed. Moreover, the risk calculus employed by some private sector entities does not adequately account for foreign cyber threats or the systemic interdependencies between different critical infrastructure sectors.

Costs. During 2014, we saw an increase in the scale and scope of reporting on malevolent cyber activity that can be measured by the amount of corporate data stolen or deleted, personally identifiable information (PII) compromised, or remediation costs incurred by US victims. For example:

- After the 2012-13 distributed denial of service (DDOS) attacks on the US financial sector, JPMorgan Chase (JPMorgan) announced plans for annual cyber security expenditures of $250 million by the end of 2014. After the company suffered a hacking intrusion in 2014, JPMorgan's CEO said he would probably double JPMorgan's annual computer security budget within the next five years.

- The 2014 data breach at Home Depot exposed information from 56 million credit/debit cards and 53 million customer email addresses. Home Depot estimated the cost of the breach to be $62 million.

- In 2014, unauthorized computer intrusions were detected on the networks of the Office of Personnel Management (OPM) as well as its contractors, US Investigations Services (USIS) and KeyPoint

Government Solutions. The two contractors were involved in processing sensitive PII related to national security clearances for Federal Government employees.

- In August 2014, the US company, Community Health Systems, informed the Securities and Exchange Commission that it believed hackers "originating from China" had stolen PII on 4.5 million individuals.

Attribution. Although cyber operators can infiltrate or disrupt targeted ICT networks, most can no longer assume that their activities will remain undetected. Nor can they assume that if detected, they will be able to conceal their identities. Governmental and private sector security professionals have made significant advances in detecting and attributing cyber intrusions.

- In May 2014, the US Department of Justice indicted five officers from China's Peoples' Liberation Army on charges of hacking US companies.

- In December 2014, computer security experts reported that members of an Iranian organization were responsible for computer operations targeting US military, transportation, public utility, and other critical infrastructure networks.

Deterrence. Numerous actors remain undeterred from conducting economic cyber espionage or perpetrating cyber attacks. The absence of universally accepted and enforceable norms of behavior in cyberspace has contributed to this situation. The motivation to conduct cyber attacks and cyber espionage will probably remain strong because of the relative ease of these operations and the gains they bring to the perpetrators. The result is a cyber environment in which multiple actors continue to test their adversaries' technical capabilities, political resolve, and thresholds. The muted response by most victims to cyber attacks has created a permissive environment in which low-level attacks can be used as a coercive tool short of war, with relatively low risk of retaliation. Additionally, even when a cyber attack can be attributed to a specific actor, the forensic attribution often requires a significant amount of time to complete. Long delays between the cyber attack and determination of attribution likewise reinforce a permissive environment.

Threat Actors

Politically motivated cyber attacks are now a growing reality, and foreign actors are reconnoitering and developing access to US critical infrastructure systems, which might be quickly exploited for disruption if an adversary's intent became hostile. In addition, those conducting cyber espionage are targeting US government, military, and commercial networks on a daily basis. These threats come from a range of actors, including: (1) nation states with highly sophisticated cyber programs (such as Russia or China), (2) nations with lesser technical capabilities but possibly more disruptive intent (such as Iran or North Korea), (3) profit-motivated criminals, and (4) ideologically motivated hackers or extremists. Distinguishing between state and non-state actors within the same country is often difficult—especially when those varied actors actively collaborate, tacitly cooperate, condone criminal activity that only harms foreign victims, or utilize similar cyber tools.

Russia. Russia's Ministry of Defense is establishing its own cyber command, which—according to senior Russian military officials—will be responsible for conducting offensive cyber activities, including propaganda operations and inserting malware into enemy command and control systems. Russia's armed forces are also establishing a specialized branch for computer network operations.

- Computer security studies assert that unspecified Russian cyber actors are developing means to access industrial control systems (ICS) remotely. These systems manage critical infrastructures such as electric power grids, urban mass-transit systems, air-traffic control, and oil and gas distribution networks. These unspecified Russian actors have successfully compromised the product supply chains of three ICS vendors so that customers download exploitative malware directly from the vendors' websites along with routine software updates, according to private sector cyber security experts.

China. Chinese economic espionage against US companies remains a significant issue. The "advanced persistent threat" activities continue despite detailed private sector reports, public indictments, and US demarches, according to a computer security study. China is an advanced cyber actor; however, Chinese hackers often use less sophisticated cyber tools to access targets. Improved cyber defenses would require hackers to use more sophisticated skills and make China's economic espionage more costly and difficult to conduct.

Iran. Iran very likely values its cyber program as one of many tools for carrying out asymmetric but proportional retaliation against political foes, as well as a sophisticated means of collecting intelligence. Iranian actors have been implicated in the 2012-13 DDOS attacks against US financial institutions and in the February 2014 cyber attack on the Las Vegas Sands casino company.

North Korea. North Korea is another state actor that uses its cyber capabilities for political objectives. The North Korean Government was responsible for the November 2014 cyber attack on Sony Pictures Entertainment (SPE), which stole corporate information and introduced hard drive erasing malware into the company's network infrastructure, according to the FBI. The attack coincided with the planned release of a SPE feature film satire that depicted the planned assassination of the North Korean president.

Terrorists. Terrorist groups will continue to experiment with hacking, which could serve as the foundation for developing more advanced capabilities. Terrorist sympathizers will probably conduct low-level cyber attacks on behalf of terrorist groups and attract attention of the media, which might exaggerate the capabilities and threat posed by these actors.

Integrity of Information

Most of the public discussion regarding cyber threats has focused on the confidentiality and availability of information; cyber espionage undermines confidentiality, whereas denial-of-service operations and data-deletion attacks undermine availability. In the future, however, we might also see more cyber operations that will change or manipulate electronic information in order to compromise its integrity (i.e. accuracy and reliability) instead of deleting it or disrupting access to it. Decisionmaking by senior government officials (civilian and military), corporate executives, investors, or others will be impaired if they cannot trust the information they are receiving.

- Successful cyber operations targeting the integrity of information would need to overcome any institutionalized checks and balances designed to prevent the manipulation of data, for example, market monitoring and clearing functions in the financial sector.

COUNTERINTELLIGENCE

We assess that the leading state intelligence threats to US interests in 2015 will continue to be Russia and China, based on their capabilities, intent, and broad operational scopes. Other states in South Asia, the Near East, and East Asia will pose increasingly sophisticated local and regional intelligence threats to US interests. For example, Iran's intelligence and security services continue to view the United States as a primary threat and have stated publicly that they monitor and counter US activities in the region.

Penetrating the US national decisionmaking apparatus and Intelligence Community will remain primary objectives for foreign intelligence entities. Additionally, the targeting of national security information and proprietary information from US companies and research institutions dealing with defense, energy, finance, dual-use technology, and other areas will be a persistent threat to US interests.

Non-state entities, including transnational organized criminals and terrorists, will continue to employ human, technical, and cyber intelligence capabilities that present a significant counterintelligence challenge. Like state intelligence services, these non-state entities recruit sources and perform physical and technical surveillance to facilitate their illegal activities and avoid detection and capture.

The internationalization of critical US supply chains and service infrastructure, including for the ICT, civil infrastructure, and national security sectors, increases the potential for subversion. This threat includes individuals, small groups of "hacktivists," commercial firms, and state intelligence services.

Trusted insiders who disclose sensitive US Government information without authorization will remain a significant threat in 2015. The technical sophistication and availability of information technology that can be used for nefarious purposes exacerbates this threat.

TERRORISM

Sunni violent extremists are gaining momentum and the number of Sunni violent extremist groups, members, and safe havens is greater than at any other point in history. These groups challenge local and regional governance and threaten US allies, partners, and interests. The threat to key US allies and partners will probably increase, but the extent of the increase will depend on the level of success that Sunni violent extremists achieve in seizing and holding territory, whether or not attacks on local regimes and calls for retaliation against the West are accepted by their key audiences, and the durability of the US-led coalition in Iraq and Syria.

Sunni violent extremists have taken advantage of fragile or unstable Muslim-majority countries to make territorial advances, seen in Syria and Iraq, and will probably continue to do so. They also contribute to regime instability and internal conflict by engaging in high levels of violence. Most will be unable to seize and hold territory on a large scale, however, as long as local, regional, and international support and resources are available and dedicated to halting their progress. The increase in the number of Sunni violent extremist groups also will probably be balanced by a lack of cohesion and authoritative leadership. Although the January 2015 attacks against Charlie Hebdo in Paris is a reminder of the threat to the West, most groups place a higher priority on local concerns than on attacking the so-called far enemy—the United States and the West—as advocated by core al- Qa'ida.

Differences in ideology and tactics will foster competition among some of these groups, particularly if a unifying figure or group does not emerge. In some cases, groups—even if hostile to each other— will ally against common enemies. For example, some Sunni violent extremists will probably gain support from like-minded insurgent or anti-regime groups or within disaffected or disenfranchised communities because they share the goal of radical regime change.

Although most homegrown violent extremists (HVEs) will probably continue to aspire to travel overseas, particularly to Syria and Iraq, they will probably remain the most likely Sunni violent extremist threat to the US homeland because of their immediate and direct access. Some might have been inspired by calls by the Islamic State of Iraq and the Levant (ISIL) in late September for individual jihadists in the West to retaliate for US-led airstrikes on ISIL. Attacks by lone actors are among the most difficult to warn about because they offer few or no signatures.

If ISIL were to substantially increase the priority it places on attacking the West rather than fighting to maintain and expand territorial control, then the group's access to radicalized Westerners who have fought in Syria and Iraq would provide a pool of operatives who potentially have access to the United States and other Western countries. Since the conflict began in 2011, more than 20,000 foreign fighters—at least 3,400 of whom are Westerners—have gone to Syria from more than 90 countries.

WEAPONS OF MASS DESTRUCTION AND PROLIFERATION

Nation-states' efforts to develop or acquire weapons of mass destruction (WMD), their delivery systems, or their underlying technologies constitute a major threat to the security of the United States, its deployed troops, and allies. Syrian regime use of chemical weapons against the opposition further demonstrates that the threat of WMD is real. The time when only a few states had access to the most dangerous technologies is past. Biological and chemical materials and technologies, almost always dual-use, move easily in the globalized economy, as do personnel with the scientific expertise to design and use them. The latest discoveries in the life sciences also diffuse rapidly around the globe.

Iran Preserving Nuclear Weapons Option

We continue to assess that Iran's overarching strategic goals of enhancing its security, prestige, and regional influence have led it to pursue capabilities to meet its civilian goals and give it the ability to build missile-deliverable nuclear weapons, if it chooses to do so. We do not know whether Iran will eventually decide to build nuclear weapons.

We also continue to assess that Iran does not face any insurmountable technical barriers to producing a nuclear weapon, making Iran's political will the central issue. However, Iranian implementation of the Joint Plan of Action (JPOA) has at least temporarily inhibited further progress in its uranium enrichment and plutonium production capabilities and effectively eliminated Iran's stockpile of 20 percent enriched uranium. The agreement has also enhanced the transparency of Iran's nuclear activities, mainly through improved International Atomic Energy Agency (IAEA) access and earlier warning of any effort to make material for nuclear weapons using its safeguarded facilities.

We judge that Tehran would choose ballistic missiles as its preferred method of delivering nuclear weapons, if it builds them. Iran's ballistic missiles are inherently capable of delivering WMD, and Tehran already has the largest inventory of ballistic missiles in the Middle East. Iran's progress on space launch vehicles—along with its desire to deter the United States and its allies—provides Tehran with the means and motivation to develop longer-range missiles, including intercontinental ballistic missiles (ICBMs).

North Korea Developing WMD-Applicable Capabilities

North Korea's nuclear weapons and missile programs pose a serious threat to the United States and to the security environment in East Asia. North Korea's export of ballistic missiles and associated materials to several countries, including Iran and Syria, and its assistance to Syria's construction of a nuclear reactor, destroyed in 2007, illustrate its willingness to proliferate dangerous technologies.

In 2013, following North Korea's third nuclear test, Pyongyang announced its intention to "refurbish and restart" its nuclear facilities, to include the uranium enrichment facility at Yongbyon, and to restart its graphite-moderated plutonium production reactor that was shut down in 2007. We assess that North Korea has followed through on its announcement by expanding its Yongbyon enrichment facility and restarting the reactor.

North Korea has also expanded the size and sophistication of its ballistic missile forces, ranging from close-range ballistic missiles to ICBMs, while continuing to conduct test launches. In 2014, North Korea launched an unprecedented number of ballistic missiles.

Pyongyang is committed to developing a long-range, nuclear-armed missile that is capable of posing a direct threat to the United States and has publicly displayed its KN08 road-mobile ICBM twice. We assess that North Korea has already taken initial steps toward fielding this system, although the system has not been flight-tested.

Because of deficiencies in their conventional military forces, North Korean leaders are focused on developing missile and WMD capabilities, particularly building nuclear weapons. Although North Korean state media regularly carries official statements on North Korea's justification for building nuclear weapons and threatening to use them as a defensive or retaliatory measure, we do not know the details of Pyongyang's nuclear doctrine or employment concepts. We have long assessed that, in Pyongyang's view, its nuclear capabilities are intended for deterrence, international prestige, and coercive diplomacy.

China's Expanding Nuclear Forces

The People's Liberation Army's (PLA's) Second Artillery Force continues to modernize its nuclear missile force by adding more survivable road-mobile systems and enhancing its silo-based systems. This new generation of missiles is intended to ensure the viability of China's strategic deterrent by providing a second strike capability. In addition, the PLA Navy continues to develop the JL-2 submarine-launched ballistic missile (SLBM) and might produce additional JIN-class nuclear-powered ballistic missile submarines. The JIN-class submarines, armed with JL-2 SLBMs, will give the PLA Navy its first long-range, sea-based nuclear capability. We assess that the Navy will soon conduct its first nuclear deterrence patrols.

Russia's New Intermediate-Range Cruise Missile

Russia has developed a new cruise missile that the United States has declared to be in violation of the Intermediate-Range Nuclear Forces (INF) Treaty. In 2013, Sergei Ivanov, a senior Russian administration official, commented in an interview how the world had changed since the time the INF Treaty was signed 1987 and noted that Russia was "developing appropriate weapons systems" in light of the proliferation of intermediate- and shorter-range ballistic missile technologies around the world. Similarly, as far back as 2007, Ivanov publicly announced that Russia had tested a ground-launched cruise missile for its Iskander weapon system, whose range complied with the INF Treaty "for now." The development of a cruise missile that is inconsistent with INF, combined with these statements about INF, calls into question Russia's commitment to this treaty.

WMD Security in Syria

In June 2014, Syria's declared CW stockpile was removed for destruction by the international community. The most hazardous chemical agents were destroyed aboard the MV CAPE RAY as of August 2014. The United States and its allies continue to work closely with the Organization for the Prohibition of Chemical Weapons (OPCW) to verify the completeness and accuracy of Syria's Chemical Weapons Convention (CWC) declaration. We judge that Syria, despite signing the treaty, has used chemicals as a means of warfare since accession to the CWC in 2013. Furthermore, the OPCW continues to investigate allegations of chlorine use in Syria.

SPACE AND COUNTERSPACE

Threats to US space systems and services will increase during 2015 and beyond as potential adversaries pursue disruptive and destructive counterspace capabilities. Chinese and Russian military leaders understand the unique information advantages afforded by space systems and services and are developing capabilities to deny access in a conflict. Chinese military writings highlight the need to interfere with, damage, and destroy reconnaissance, navigation, and communication satellites. China has satellite jamming capabilities and is pursuing antisatellite systems. In July 2014, China conducted a non-destructive antisatellite missile test. China conducted a previous destructive test of the system in 2007, which created long-lived space debris. Russia's 2010 Military Doctrine emphasizes space defense as a vital component of its national defense. Russian leaders openly assert that the Russian armed forces have antisatellite weapons and conduct antisatellite research. Russia has satellite jammers and is pursuing antisatellite systems.

TRANSNATIONAL ORGANIZED CRIME

Transnational Organized Crime (TOC) is a global, persistent threat to our communities at home and our interests abroad. Savvy, profit-driven criminal networks traffic in drugs, persons, wildlife, and weapons; corrode security and governance; undermine legitimate economic activity and the rule of law; cost economies important revenue; and undercut US development efforts.

Drug Trafficking

Drug trafficking will remain a major TOC threat to the United States. Mexico is the largest foreign producer of US-bound marijuana, methamphetamines, and heroin, and the conduit for the overwhelming majority of US-bound cocaine from South America. The drug trade also undermines US interests abroad, eroding stability in parts of Africa and Latin America; Afghanistan accounts for 80 percent of the world's opium production. Weak Central American states will continue to be the primary transit area for the majority of US-bound cocaine. The Caribbean is becoming an increasingly important secondary transit area for US- and European-bound cocaine. In 2013, the world's capacity to produce heroin reached the second highest level in nearly 20 years, increasing the likelihood that the drug will remain accessible and inexpensive in consumer markets in the United States, where heroin-related deaths have surged since 2007. New psychoactive substances (NPS), including synthetic cannabinoids and synthetic cathinones, pose an emerging and rapidly growing global public health threat. Since 2009, US law enforcement officials have encountered more than 240 synthetic compounds. Worldwide, 348 new psychoactive substances had been identified, exceeding the number of 234 illicit substances under international controls.

Criminals Profiting from Global Instability

Transnational criminal organizations will continue to exploit opportunities in ongoing conflicts to destabilize societies, economies, and governance. Regional unrest, population displacements, endemic corruption, and political turmoil will provide openings that criminals will exploit for profit and to improve their standing relative to other power brokers.

Corruption

Corruption facilitates transnational organized crime and vice versa. Both phenomena exacerbate other threats to local, regional, and international security. Corruption exists at some level in all countries; however, the symbiotic relationship between government officials and TOC networks is particularly pernicious in some countries. One example is Russia, where the nexus among organized crime, state actors, and business blurs the distinction between state policy and private gain.

Human Trafficking

Human trafficking remains both a human rights concern and a challenge to international security. Trafficking in persons has become a lucrative source of revenue—estimated to produce tens of billions of dollars annually. Human traffickers leverage corrupt officials, porous borders, and lax enforcement to ply their illicit trade. This exploitation of human lives for profit continues to occur in every country in the world—undermining the rule of law and corroding legitimate institutions of government and commerce.

Wildlife Trafficking

Illicit trade in wildlife, timber, and marine resources endangers the environment, threatens rule of law and border security in fragile regions, and destabilizes communities that depend on wildlife for biodiversity and ecotourism. Increased demand for ivory and rhino horn in Asia has triggered unprecedented increases in poaching in Africa. Criminal elements, often in collusion with corrupt government officials or security forces, are involved in poaching and movement of ivory and rhino horn across Africa. Poaching presents significant security challenges for militaries and police forces in African nations, which often are outgunned by poachers and their allies. Illegal, unreported, and unregulated fishing threatens food security and the preservation of marine resources. It often occurs concurrently with forced labor in the fishing industry.

Theft of Cultural Properties, Artifacts. and Antiquities

Although the theft and trafficking of cultural heritage and art are traditions as old as the cultures they represent, transnational organized criminals are acquiring, transporting, and selling valuable cultural property and art more swiftly, easily, and stealthily. These criminals operate on a global scale without regard for laws, borders, nationalities or the significance of the treasures they smuggle.

ECONOMICS AND NATURAL RESOURCES

The global economy continues to adjust to and recover from the global financial crisis that began in 2008; economic growth since that period is lagging behind that of the previous decade. Resumption of sustained growth has been elusive for many of the world's largest economies, particularly in European countries and Japan. The prospect of diminished or forestalled recoveries in these developed economies as well as disappointing growth in key developing countries has contributed to a readjustment of energy and commodity markets.

Energy and Commodities

Energy prices experienced sharp declines during the second half of 2014. Diminishing global growth prospects, OPEC's decision to maintain its output levels, rapid increases in unconventional oil production in Canada and the United States, and the partial resumption of some previously sidelined output in Libya and elsewhere helped drive down prices by more than half since July, the first substantial decline since 2008-09. Lower-priced oil and gas will give a boost to the global economy, with benefits enjoyed by importers more than outweighing the costs to exporters.

Macroeconomic Stability

Extraordinary monetary policy or "quantitative easing" has helped revive growth in the United States since the global financial crisis. However, this recovery and the prospect of higher returns in the United States will probably continue to draw investment capital from the rest of the world, where weak growth has left interest rates depressed.

Global output improved slightly in 2014 but continued to lag the growth rates seen before 2008. Since 2008, the worldwide GDP growth rate has averaged about 3.2 percent, well below its 20-year, pre-GFC average of 3.9 percent. Looking ahead, prospects for slowing economic growth in Europe and China do not bode well for the global economic environment.

Economic growth has been inconsistent among developed and developing economies alike. Outside of the largest economies—the United States, the EU, and China—economic growth largely stagnated worldwide in 2014, slowing to 2.1 percent. As a result, the difference in growth rates of developing countries and developed countries continued to narrow—to 2.6 percentage points. This gap, smallest in more than a decade, underscores the continued weakness in emerging markets, whose previously much-higher average growth rates helped drive global growth.

HUMAN SECURITY

Critical Trends Converging

Several trends are converging that will probably increase the frequency of shocks to human security in 2015. Emerging infectious diseases and deficiencies in international state preparedness to address them remain a threat, exemplified by the epidemic spread of the Ebola virus in West Africa. Extremes in weather combined with public policies that affect food and water supplies will probably exacerbate humanitarian crises. Many states and international institutions will look to the United States in 2015 for leadership to address human security issues, particularly environment and global health, as well as those caused by poor or abusive governance.

Global trends in governance are negative and portend growing instability. Poor and abusive governance threatens the security and rights of individuals and civil society in many countries throughout the world. The overall risk for mass atrocities—driven in part by increasing social mobilization, violent conflict, and a diminishing quality of governance—is growing. Incidents of religious persecution also are on the rise. Legal restrictions on NGOs and the press, particularly those that expose government shortcomings or lobby for reforms, will probably continue.

Infectious Disease Continues To Threaten Human Security Worldwide

Infectious diseases are among the foremost health security threats. A more crowded and interconnected world is increasing the opportunities for human and animal diseases to emerge and spread globally. This has been demonstrated by the emergence of Ebola in West Africa on an unprecedented scale. In addition, military conflicts and displacement of populations with loss of basic infrastructure can lead to spread of disease. Climate change can also lead to changes in the distribution of vectors for diseases.

- The Ebola outbreak, which began in late 2013 in a remote area of Guinea, quickly spread into neighboring Liberia and Sierra Leone and then into dense urban transportation hubs, where it began spreading out of control. Gaps in disease surveillance and reporting, limited health care resources, and other factors contributed to the outpacing of the international community's response in West Africa. Isolated Ebola cases appeared outside of the most affected countries—notably in Spain and the United States—and the disease will almost certainly continue in 2015 to threaten regional economic stability, security, and governance.

- Antimicrobial drug resistance is increasingly threatening global health security. Seventy percent of known bacteria have acquired resistance to at least one antibiotic that is used to treat infections, threatening a return to the pre-antibiotic era. Multidrug-resistant tuberculosis has emerged in China, India, Russia, and elsewhere. During the next twenty years, antimicrobial drug-resistant pathogens will probably continue to increase in number and geographic scope, worsening health outcomes, straining public health budgets, and harming US interests throughout the world.

- MERS, a novel virus from the same family as SARS, emerged in 2012 in Saudi Arabia. Isolated cases migrated to Southeast Asia, Europe, and the United States. Cases of highly pathogenic influenza are also continuing to appear in different regions of the world. HIV/AIDS and malaria, although trending downward, remain global health priorities. In 2013, 2.1 million people were newly infected with HIV and 584,000 were killed by malaria, according to the World Health Organization. Diarrheal diseases like cholera continue to take the lives of 800,000 children annually.

- The world's population remains vulnerable to infectious diseases because anticipating which pathogen might spread from animals to humans or if a human virus will take a more virulent form is nearly impossible. For example, if a highly pathogenic avian influenza virus like H7N9 were to become easily transmissible among humans, the outcome could be far more disruptive than the great influenza pandemic of 1918. It could lead to global economic losses, the unseating of governments, and disturbance of geopolitical alliances.

Extreme Weather Exacerbating Risks to Global Food and Water Security

Extreme weather, climate change, and public policies that affect food and water supplies will probably create or exacerbate humanitarian crises and instability risks. Globally averaged surface temperature rose approximately 0.8 degrees Celsius (about 1.4 degrees Fahrenheit) from 1951 to 2014; 2014 was warmest on earth since recordkeeping began. This rise in temperature has probably caused an increase in the intensity and frequency of both heavy precipitation and prolonged heat waves and has changed the spread of certain diseases. This trend will probably continue. Demographic and development trends that concentrate people in cities—often along coasts—will compound and amplify the impact of extreme weather and climate change on populations. Countries whose key systems—food, water, energy, shelter, transportation, and medical—are resilient will be better able to avoid significant economic and human losses from extreme weather.

- Global food supplies will probably be adequate for 2015 but are becoming increasingly fragile in Africa, the Middle East, and South Asia. The risks of worsening food insecurity in regions of strategic importance to the United States will increase because of threats to local food availability, lower purchasing power, and counterproductive government policies. Price shocks will result if extreme weather or disease patterns significantly reduce food production in multiple areas of the world, especially in key exporting countries.

- Risks to freshwater supplies—due to shortages, poor quality, floods, and climate change—are growing. These problems hinder the ability of countries to produce food and generate energy, potentially undermining global food markets and hobbling economic growth. Combined with demographic and economic development pressures, such problems will particularly hinder the efforts of North Africa, the Middle East, and South Asia to cope with their water problems. Lack of adequate water might be a destabilizing factor in countries that lack the management mechanisms, financial resources, political will, or technical ability to solve their internal water problems.

- Some states are heavily dependent on river water controlled by upstream nations. When upstream water infrastructure development threatens downstream access to water, states might attempt to exert pressure on their neighbors to preserve their water interests. Such pressure might be applied in international forums and also includes pressing investors, nongovernmental organizations, and donor countries to support or halt water infrastructure projects. Some countries will almost certainly construct and support major water projects. Over the longer term, wealthier developing countries will also probably face increasing water-related social disruptions. Developing countries, however, are almost certainly capable of addressing water problems without risk of state failure. Terrorist organizations might also increasingly seek to control or degrade water infrastructure to gain revenue or influence populations.

Increase in Global Instability Risk

Global political instability risks will remain high in 2015 and beyond. Mass atrocities, sectarian or religious violence, and curtailed NGO activities will all continue to increase these risks. Declining economic conditions are contributing to risk of instability or internal conflict.

- Roughly half of the world's countries not already experiencing or recovering from instability are in the "most risk" and "significant risk" categories for regime-threatening and violent instability through 2015.

- Overall international will and capability to prevent or mitigate mass atrocities will probably diminish in 2015 owing to reductions in government budgets and spending.

- In 2014, about two dozen countries increased restrictions on NGOs. Approximately another dozen also plan to do so in 2015, according to the International Center for Nonprofit Law.

REGIONAL THREATS

MIDDLE EAST AND NORTH AFRICA

Iraq

Over six months into the coalition campaign against the Islamic State of Iraq and the Levant (ISIL), the frontlines against the group in Iraq have largely stabilized; no side is able to muster the resources necessary to attain its territorial ambitions. The Iraqi Security Forces (ISF), Peshmerga, Shia militants, and a few tribal allies—bolstered by air and artillery strikes, weapons, and advice from the United States, Arab and Western allies, and Iran—have prevented ISIL from gaining large swaths of additional territory.

Sectarian conflict in mixed Shia-Sunni areas in and around Baghdad that can undermine progress against ISIL is growing. ISF and Shia militants are conducting a campaign of retribution killings and forced displacement of Sunni civilians in several areas contested by Sunni militants.

Since taking office, Prime Minister al-Abadi has taken steps to change the ethno-sectarian tone in Baghdad, including engaging Sunni tribal leaders and reaching a tentative oil agreement with the Kurdistan Regional Government. However, the ethnosectarian nature of security operations and persistent distrust among Iraqi leaders risk undermining Abadi's nascent political progress.

Syria

The Syrian regime made consistent gains in 2014 in parts of western Syria that it considers key, retaking ground in eastern Damascus, Homs, and Latakia; it is close to surrounding Aleppo city. The regime will require years to reassert significant control over the country.

- The bulk of the opposition in the north is fighting on three fronts—against the regime, the al-Qa'ida-affiliated Nusrah Front, and ISIL. The opposition in the south has made steady gains in areas that the regime has not made a priority and where ISIL has only a limited presence.

The stability of Syria's neighbors is at risk due to the country's prolonged conflict, which will strain regional economies forced to absorb millions of refugees. The conflict will also encourage regional sectarianism and continue to incubate extremist groups that will use Syria as a launching pad for attacks across the Middle East.

- The Syrian conflict is also putting huge economic and resource strains on countries in the region primarily due to the nearly 4 million refugees fleeing the conflict. Most of the refugees have fled to neighboring states. More than 620,000 are in Jordan; almost 1.6 million are in Turkey; almost 1.2 million are in Lebanon; and more than 240,000 are in Iraq. These states have requested additional international support to manage the influx.

Islamic State of Iraq and the Levant

In an attempt to strengthen its self-declared caliphate, ISIL probably plans to conduct operations against regional allies, Western facilities, and personnel in the Middle East; it has already executed Western and Japanese hostages as well as a Jordanian Air Force pilot. ISIL leader Abu Bakr al-Baghdadi outlined the group's ambitious external goals, including the expansion of the caliphate into the Arabian Peninsula and North Africa and attacks against Western, regional, and Shia interests, according to a public statement in November 2014.

- In September 2014, ISIL publicly called on all Sunnis to retaliate for US-led airstrikes in Iraq and Syria, advocating the targeting of law enforcement and other government officials using any means available. Individuals from Europe and North America who have trained and fought with ISIL can return home and conduct attacks either on their own or on ISIL's behalf. The French citizen arrested in May 2014 for a shooting at a Jewish museum in Brussels had returned from fighting, probably with ISIL in Syria, and was wrapped in a flag with ISIL inscriptions when he was apprehended. We do not know whether he acted at ISIL's behest.

Iran

The Islamic Republic of Iran is an ongoing threat to US national interests because of its support to the Asad regime in Syria, promulgation of anti-Israeli policies, development of advanced military capabilities, and pursuit of its nuclear program. President Ruhani—a longstanding member of the regime establishment—will not depart from Iran's national security objectives of protecting the regime and enhancing Iranian influence abroad, even while attempting different approaches to achieve these goals. He requires Supreme Leader Khamenei's support to continue engagement with the West, moderate foreign policy, and ease social restrictions within Iran.

Iran possesses a substantial inventory of theater ballistic missiles capable of reaching as far as some areas of southeastern Europe. Tehran is developing increasingly sophisticated missiles and improving the range and accuracy of its other missile systems. Iran is also acquiring advanced naval and aerospace capabilities, including naval mines, small but capable submarines, coastal defense cruise missile batteries, attack craft, anti-ship missiles, and armed unmanned aerial vehicles.

In Iraq and Syria, Iran seeks to preserve friendly governments, protect Shia interests, defeat Sunni extremists, and marginalize US influence. The rise of ISIL has prompted Iran to devote more resources to blunting Sunni extremist advances that threaten Iran's regional allies and interests. Iran's security services have provided robust military support to Baghdad and Damascus, including arms, advisers, funding, and direct combat support. Both conflicts have allowed Iran to gain valuable on-the-ground experience in counterinsurgency operations. Iranian assistance has been instrumental in expanding the capabilities of Shia militants in Iraq. The ISIL threat has also reduced Iraqi resistance to integrating those militants, with Iranian help, into the Iraqi Security Forces, but Iran has uneven control over these groups.

Despite Iran's intentions to dampen sectarianism, build responsive partners, and deescalate tensions with Saudi Arabia, Iranian leaders—particularly within the security services—are pursuing policies with negative secondary consequences for regional stability and potentially for Iran. Iran's actions to protect and empower Shia communities are fueling growing fears and sectarian responses.

Libya

We assess that Libya will remain volatile in 2015. Political polarization and broadening militia violence have pushed Libya into a civil war. Nearly four years since the revolution that toppled Qadhafi, rival governments have emerged, leaving the country with no clear legitimate political authority or credible security forces. Militias aligned with the rival governments continue to vie for dominance in Tripoli and Benghazi.

- In Benghazi, fighting that began in May 2014 is ongoing between forces aligned with former General Khalifa Hafar's Operation Dignity forces and Ansar al-Sharia (AAS) and allied groups. In Tripoli, the Libya Dawn militias have driven their Zintani militia rivals out of the city, but fighting continues southwest of Tripoli.

- UN efforts to facilitate a negotiated resolution between Libya's rival governments have shown limited momentum but as of early February 2015 have not made tangible progress toward a unity government or a durable cease-fire.

Extremists and terrorists from al-Qa'ida-affiliated and allied groups are using Libya's permissive security environment as a safe haven to plot attacks, including against Western interests in Libya and the region. ISIL also has declared the country part of its caliphate, and ISIL-aligned extremists are trying to institute *sharia* in parts of the country.

Yemen

The Huthis have emerged as the most powerful group in Yemen since taking Sanaa last fall and are poised to dominate the political process after President's Hadi's resignation and their dissolution of the government. The group, however, continues to face resistance as it expands toward the south and east. Southern Yemeni leaders have been alarmed by the Huthi's consolidation of control in Sanaa and are poised to oppose further Huthi expansion south. Al-Qa'ida in the Arabian Peninsula (AQAP) has taken advantage of many Sunni tribes' opposition to Huthi expansion to gain recruits to fight against the Huthis.

Chronic and severe economic and humanitarian problems, exacerbated by repeated pipeline attacks and the Huthis' push to reinstate costly fuel subsidies, will continue to undercut government control and legitimacy. Yemen will probably continue pressuring donor nations to make good on aid pledges while negotiating with tribes outside of Sanaa's control to keep oil exports flowing.

Huthi ascendency in Yemen has increased Iran's influence as well.

Lebanon

Lebanon continues to struggle with spillover from the Syrian conflict, including periodic sectarian violence; terrorist attacks; and the economic, political, and sectarian strain associated with refugees.

- Lebanon faces growing threats from terrorist groups, including the al-Nusrah Front and ISIL. Sunni extremists are trying to establish networks in Lebanon and have increased attacks against Lebanese army and Hizballah positions along the Lebanese-Syrian border. Lebanon potentially faces a protracted conflict in northern and eastern parts of the country from extremist groups seeking to seize Lebanese territory, supplies, and hostages.

- The presence of over one million mostly Sunni Syrian refugees in Lebanon, which has a population of only 4.1 million, has significantly altered Lebanon's sectarian demographics and is a continuing burden on the Lebanese economy. In October 2014, the cabinet further tightened entry restrictions to allow only "extreme humanitarian cases" into the country. Arrivals have declined 75 to 90 percent since August, most recently due in part to the new restrictions.

Egypt

Egyptian officials have announced that legislative elections will start in March 2015 and that voting will be staggered in phases over seven weeks. Egypt faces a persistent threat of terrorist and militant violence that is directed primarily at the state security forces both in the Sinai Peninsula and mainland Egypt. Since mid-2013, Sinai-based terrorist group Ansar Bayt al-Maqdis (ABM)—affiliated since November with ISIL—has claimed responsibility for some of the most sophisticated and deadly attacks against Egyptian security forces in decades.

Tunisia

Tunisia has transitioned to a permanent democratic government. Beji Caid Essebsi was elected President in the presidential runoff election in December 2014. In January 2015, Essebsi's political party Nidaa Tounes selected former Interior Minister Essid to become Prime Minister.

- In early February, Prime Minister Habib Essid formed a broad-based coalition government, led by Nidaa Tounes, which included Islamist party al-Nahda and several smaller parties. The new government almost certainly recognizes Tunisia's economic and security challenges.

The permanent government will inherit one of the highest youth unemployment rates in the world, a high budget deficit, and decreasing Foreign Direct Investment and balance of payments. It will struggle to meet public expectations for swift economic progress.

EUROPE

Turkey

Turkey will remain a critical partner in a wide range of US security policy priorities, including anti-ISIL and broader counterterrorism efforts. Joint US-Turkish efforts to stem instability in Iraq and Syria share the same goals but employ different approaches, increasing tension in the bilateral relationship. Turkish President Erdogan and leaders of the ruling Justice and Development Party (AKP) are focused on the general elections, which are scheduled to be held in June 2015.

- Ankara will be more inclined to support the anti-ISIL coalition if the coalition agrees to focus efforts against Asad, including setting up an internationally guaranteed buffer zone in Syria.

- Turkey is concerned that the Kurdish Democratic Union (PYD)—a group it believes is affiliated with the Kurdistan People's Congress (KGK/former PKK)—will gain international legitimacy.

Key Partners

The Transatlantic partnership remains vital as the United States works with European leaders to maintain a concerted response to Russia's action in Ukraine and to other security challenges on the European continent and beyond. Europeans are working to address fiscal challenges and encourage economic growth while maintaining and strengthening financial governance.

- The Transatlantic Trade and Investment Partnership has the potential to help generate economic growth for both the United States and Europe, reinforce the transatlantic link, and address public concerns about data privacy and food and health standards.

RUSSIA AND EURASIA

Russia

The Ukrainian crisis has profoundly affected Russia's relations with the West and will have far-reaching effects on Russia's domestic politics, economic development, and foreign policy.

President Vladimir Putin enjoys some of his highest domestic approval ratings in all his years in office. An intense state media propaganda campaign has stoked Russians' perception that Putin righted a historical wrong in orchestrating Russia's seizure of Crimea and reasserted Russia's great-power interests against a hostile West.

At the same time, the crisis in Ukraine has exacerbated preexisting domestic problems in Russia. The fall of former Ukrainian President Viktor Yanukovych's government in February 2014 has almost certainly deepened the Kremlin's concerns over the dangers of mass demonstrations and has intensified the Kremlin's efforts to defuse what it sees as potential catalysts for protests in Russia.

Russia's economy was in decline even before the crisis began. Growth stagnated in 2014 due to declining oil prices, large capital outflows, and a sharply declining ruble. In addition, economic sanctions cut off some Russian firms from Western financing. These factors have increased the real and perceived risks of doing business in Russia, raised the overall cost of international credit, and will probably drive Russia into recession in 2015.

Moscow is pushing for greater regional integration, pressing neighboring states to follow the example of Belarus and Kazakhstan and join the Moscow-led Eurasian Economic Union. The Kremlin is also cultivating its relationship with China, seeking to maintain some influence in Europe and emphasizing multilateral forums to counter what Moscow views as US unilateralism. These trends were already present in Russian diplomacy, but the Ukrainian crisis has almost certainly lent emphasis to these policies.

Russia is taking information warfare to a new level, working to fan anti-US and anti-Western sentiment both within Russia and globally. Russian state-controlled media publish false and misleading information in an effort to discredit the West, undercut consensus on Russia, and build sympathy for Russian positions.

In Ukraine, Russia has demonstrated its willingness to covertly use military and paramilitary forces in a neighboring state—a development that raises anxieties in states along Russia's periphery. Future Russian deployments and force posture changes will probably be designed to maximize their diplomatic and public impact in Europe. Russian military officials have announced plans to conduct more "out-of-area" air and naval deployments, to include greater activity in the Caribbean and Mediterranean Seas.

Moscow has made headway in modernizing its nuclear and conventional forces, improving its training and joint operational proficiency, modernizing its military doctrine to integrate new methods of warfare, and developing long-range, precision-strike capabilities. Despite its economic difficulties, Moscow is committed to modernizing its military.

Ukraine, Moldova, and Belarus

Ukraine faces a daunting array of problems after nearly a year of conflict with Russia and its proxies in eastern Ukraine. At the same time, the crisis has fostered a sense of national identity and unity. Public opinion has shifted heavily in favor of pursuing integration with the EU while views of Russia have become sharply negative. Moreover, for the first time, a narrow majority of the population supports NATO membership.

Negotiations over the status of the separatist-held territory in eastern Ukraine will almost certainly be difficult and protracted. Russia has supplied substantial quantities of heavy weapons to strengthen the separatists' forces and covertly supports them with its own troops, both within Ukraine and from across the border. More importantly, Moscow has demonstrated that it is willing to intervene directly to prevent the separatists from being defeated on the battlefield. Further fighting is likely in 2015.

Ukraine's dire economic situation presents no less a challenge to Kyiv than the conflict in the east. Ukraine will be highly dependent on substantial outside financial assistance for years to come.

In **Moldova**, the narrow victory of pro-EU parties in the latest parliamentary elections suggests that Moldova will push ahead with its European integration agenda. However, Chisinau still faces numerous challenges in seeking to overcome economic difficulties, entrenched corruption, and Moscow's displeasure with Moldova's rejection of closer integration with Russia. Any progress on resolving the political status of the ethnic-Russian separatist region of Transnistria is unlikely.

On 1 January 2015, **Belarus** became, along with Kazakhstan, a founding member of the Eurasian Economic Union (EEU), a regional integration project that Moscow eventually plans to transform into a Eurasian Union as a counterpart to the EU. President Lukashenko has tread carefully in regard to the

Ukrainian crisis, declining to recognize Russia's seizure of Crimea, but agreeing nevertheless to deepen military cooperation with Moscow.

The Caucasus and Central Asia

In **Georgia**, progress is unlikely on the core disputes between Tbilisi and Moscow, including Georgia's NATO aspirations and the status of the occupied territories of Abkhazia and South Ossetia. Tensions with Russia will remain high, and we assess that Moscow will press Tbilisi to abandon closer EU and NATO ties.

Armenia and **Azerbaijan** saw an increase in 2014 of ceasefire violations and a record number of casualties along the Line of Contact (LOC), which separates ethnic Armenian and Azerbaijani forces near the separatist region of Nagorno-Karabakh. The increased violence highlights how the close proximity of opposing military forces continues to pose a risk of miscalculation and unintended escalation. Prospects for a peaceful resolution in the foreseeable future are dim.

Central Asian states remain concerned about regional instability in light of a reduced Coalition presence in Afghanistan. Although they have long been alarmed about the activities of Central Asian militant groups operating in Afghanistan and Pakistan, they are increasingly worried about the threat posed by the return of the small but growing number of their nationals who have traveled to Syria to join violent Islamist extremist groups. On the whole, however, the Central Asian states will probably face more acute risks of instability in 2015 from internal issues such as unclear political succession plans, weak economies, ethnic tensions, and political repression—any of which could produce a crisis with little warning.

EAST ASIA

China

China will continue to pursue an active foreign policy—especially within the Asia Pacific—bolstered by increasing capabilities and its firm stance on East and South China Sea territorial disputes with rival claimants. The chances for sustained tensions will persist because competing claimants will probably pursue actions—including energy exploration—that others perceive as infringing on their sovereignty. China will probably seek to expand its economic role and outreach in the region, pursuing broader acceptance of its economic initiatives, including the Asia Infrastructure Investment Bank. Although China remains focused on regional issues, it will seek a greater voice on major international issues and in making new international rules.

Notwithstanding this external agenda, Chinese leaders will focus primarily on addressing domestic concerns. The Chinese Communist Party leadership under President Xi Jinping announced an ambitious agenda of legal reforms in late 2014 that built on its previous agenda of ambitious economic reforms—all aimed at improving government efficiency and accountability and strengthening the control of the Communist Party. The difficulty of implementing these reforms and bureaucratic resistance to them create the possibility of rising internal frictions as the agenda moves forward. Beijing will also remain concerned about the potential for domestic unrest or terrorist acts in Xinjiang and Tibet, which might lead to renewed human rights abuses. Following months of pro-democracy protests in late 2014, Chinese leaders will monitor closely political developments in Hong Kong for signs of instability.

North Korea

Three years after taking the helm of North Korea, Kim Jong Un has further solidified his position as unitary leader and final decision authority through purges, executions, and leadership shuffles. Kim was absent from public view for 40 days in late 2014, leading to widespread foreign media speculation about his health and the regime's stability. The focus on Kim's health is a reminder that the regime's stability might hinge on Kim's personal status. Kim has no clearly identified successor and is inclined to prevent the emergence of a clear "number two" who could consolidate power in his absence. Kim and the regime have publicly emphasized his focus on improving the country's troubled economy and the livelihood of the North Korean people while maintaining the tenets of a command economy. He has codified this approach via his dual-track policy of economic development and advancement of nuclear weapons. (Information on North Korea's nuclear weapons program and intentions can be found above in the section on WMD and Proliferation.) Despite renewed efforts at diplomatic outreach, Kim continues to challenge the international community with provocative and threatening behavior in pursuit of his goals, as prominently demonstrated in the November 2014 cyber attack on Sony.

SOUTH ASIA

Afghanistan

President Ashraf Ghani and Chief Executive Officer Abdullah Abdullah secured Parliament's approval of the Bilateral Security Agreement and NATO Status of Forces Agreement prior to the NATO Ministerial in December 2014. Despite the 12 January announcement of their cabinet nominees, Ghani and Abdullah have yet to win legislative approval for all of those nominated or resolve the final details of their shared political powers derived from their national unity government agreement. Resolving these issues will require continued international engagement and support.

International financial aid remains the most important external determinant of the Kabul government's strength. However, the slow economic recovery from the global financial crisis has created fiscal challenges for many of Afghanistan's primary donors, particularly in Europe and Japan. These economic hurdles at home have reduced donors' enthusiasm and capacity to provide Afghanistan additional long-term financial aid above levels pledged through 2017 and reaffirmed in 2014 at the London Conference and NATO Wales Summit.

The Afghan National Security Forces (ANSF) prevented the Taliban from achieving a decisive military advantage in 2014. The ANSF, however, will require continued international security sector support and funding to stave off an increasingly aggressive Taliban insurgency through 2015. The ANSF, with the help of anti-Taliban powerbrokers and international funding, will probably maintain control of most major population centers. However, the forces will most likely cede control of some rural areas. Without international funding, the ANSF will probably not remain a cohesive or viable force.

The Taliban will probably remain largely cohesive under the leadership of Mullah Omar and sustain its countrywide campaign to take territory in outlying areas and steadily reassert influence over significant portions of the Pashtun countryside, positioning itself for greater territorial gains in 2015. Reliant on Afghanistan's opiate trade as a key domestic source of funding, the Taliban will be able to exploit increasing opium poppy cultivation and potential heroin production for ready revenue. The Taliban has publicly touted the end of the mission of the International Security and Assistance Force (ISAF) and coalition drawdown as a sign of its inevitable victory, reinforcing its commitment to returning to power.

Pakistan

Pakistan will probably continue to implement some economic reforms and target anti-Pakistan militants and their activities.

- Prime Minister Sharif's promises to address economic, energy, and security issues almost certainly fell short of high public expectations. Furthermore, his standing weakened when he reportedly asked the Army to step in and handle opposition protests in late 2014.

- We assess that Islamabad will approve some additional economic reforms in 2015. Undertaking future economic and energy reforms will be more challenging and will probably face greater political and popular opposition.

- The Pakistan Government will probably focus in 2015 on diminishing the capabilities of the Tehrik-i-Taliban (TTP), which claimed the attack on a school in December—leaving over 100 children dead.

We judge that Pakistan will aim to establish positive rapport with the new Afghan Government, but longstanding distrust and unresolved disputes between the countries will prevent substantial progress.

- Pakistan's provision of safe haven to Lashkar-e Tayyiba will probably continue to be a key irritant in relations with India.

India

Prime Minister Narendra Modi's decisive leadership style, combined with the 2014 election of an absolute majority in the lower house of Parliament of his Bharatiya Janata Party (BJP), will enable more decisive Indian decisionmaking on domestic and foreign policy. Although India has a long-standing position that it maintain an independent policy, Modi will probably seek to work more closely with the United States on security, terrorism, and economic issues.

India wants to maintain a stable peace with Pakistan but views Pakistan as a direct terrorism threat and a regional source of instability.

India is concerned about the stability of Afghanistan and its own presence there following the drawdown of international forces and is looking for options to blunt the influence of Pakistani-supported groups and ensure that Afghanistan does not revert to a haven for anti-Indian militants.

Indian leaders will almost certainly pursue stronger economic ties with China that support the government's economic agenda of closing the trade gap and attracting investment in infrastructure. New Delhi's concern over perceived Chinese aggressiveness along the disputed border and in the Indian Ocean is probably growing in light of border incidents and the visit of a Chinese submarine to Sri Lanka in 2014.

SUB-SAHARAN AFRICA

Sub-Saharan Africa will face political and security challenges in 2015 including numerous presidential elections, ongoing insurgencies, and continuing intrastate conflict. The ongoing Ebola virus epidemic will undoubtedly challenge both Western African nations and the larger international community in trying to contain the virus' spread and counter economic degradation in fragile West African nations. Stability in South Sudan, Nigeria, Somalia, and the Central African Republic (CAR) will almost certainly remain tenuous throughout 2015.

West Africa

The Ebola virus will persist throughout West Africa in 2015, posing a significant threat to the economic viability and consequently the stability of the region. The continued drain on resources and unprecedented need for medical personnel will strain governments and economies in Liberia, Sierra Leone, and Guinea—the three worst-affected countries. Sustained financial and materiel assistance from the international community, continued domestic support for the governments' anti-Ebola efforts, and community engagement to change local misperceptions about the disease's cause, treatment options, and burial practices will remain critical to slowing the epidemic. Economic growth in the outbreak zone has already slowed and will continue to slow during 2015, straining budgets and probably increasing dependence on international donor aid. A prolonged or severe outbreak that continues well into 2015 might prompt Guinea to delay Presidential elections, increasing the possibility of election-related violence. Military and security services in the key outbreak countries will probably successfully contain isolated unrest and local hostility toward Ebola-response personnel.

Sudan

Khartoum will almost certainly confront a range of challenges, including continued insurgencies in the periphery, public dissatisfaction over continued economic decline, and potential protests surrounding its April 2015 elections. Sudanese economic conditions since South Sudan's independence in 2011 continue to deteriorate. Such conditions, including rising prices on staple goods, fuel opposition to the Sudanese Government.

South Sudan

Clashes between opposition forces and the Sudan People's Liberation Army (SPLA) will almost certainly increase during the dry season—which lasts from November to April—undermining ongoing peace talks and putting tenuous humanitarian gains at risk. Peace talks between Juba and opposition elements will probably remain slow-going.

Nigeria

Instability in Nigeria will probably increase in 2015, given contentious elections delayed until March and April, plummeting oil revenue, and the military's inability to check Boko Haram's ascendancy in the northeast. The election will occasion violence, with prospects for protests in the months following the election. In addition, militants might remobilize in the Niger Delta and attack the oil industry. Boko Haram will probably continue to solidify control over its self-declared Islamic state in northeastern Nigeria and expand its terror campaign in neighboring Nigerian states, Cameroon, Niger, and Chad. Abuja's reliance on oil exports for revenue will almost certainly ensure that Nigeria remains vulnerable to fluctuations in the global oil market in 2015. Declining oil prices will probably squeeze government revenues and drain currency reserves. Abuja's overtaxed security forces will have a limited ability to anticipate and preempt threats.

Somalia

In Somalia, al-Shabaab is conducting asymmetric attacks against government facilities and Western targets in and around Mogadishu. The credibility and effectiveness of the young Somali Government will be further threatened by persistent political infighting; ill-equipped government institutions; and pervasive technical, political, and administrative shortfalls.

Lord's Resistance Army

The Lord's Resistance Army (LRA), even in its weakened state, probably has the ability to regenerate if counter-LRA operations are reduced. The LRA continues to display great agility in its geographic areas of operation and in the operational security of its activities.

Central African Republic

Despite the presence of international peacekeeping forces, the risk of continued ethno-religious clashes between Christians and Muslims throughout the country, including in the capital, remains high.

The Sahel

Governments in Africa's Sahel region—particularly Chad, Niger, Mali, and Mauritania—will remain at risk of terrorist attacks and possible internal conflict. Al-Qa'ida in the Lands of the Islamic Maghreb (AQIM) and affiliated groups are committed to continuing their terrorist activity in the Sahel, including against Western interests. They will probably seek to increase the frequency and scale of attacks in northern Mali. Sahelien militaries will struggle to handle a wide array of security threats.

LATIN AMERICA AND THE CARIBBEAN

Cuba

Cuban President Raul Castro's focus will almost certainly be preparing the country for the eventual end of the Castro era and maintaining tight political control. He is cautiously implementing economic and leadership reforms and released dozens of political prisoners in early January. Cuba's principal interest in normalizing relations with the United States is probably linked to its recognition of the need to ease discontent over dismal living conditions and poor economic prospects. The slow rollout of economic reforms and a fall in nickel output cut GDP growth to 1.2 percent in 2014. Crucial components of the economic reform program—reducing the state role in the economy and opening up a few opportunities for self-employment—will probably produce numerous, short-term economic dislocations before gradually increasing productivity and jobs.

Cuba's population of 11 million has been declining since about 2005 because of falling birthrates and emigration. Cuban migrant arrivals at the US southwest border rose from 10,400 in FY12 to 17,300 in FY14. Maritime arrivals and interdictions will probably increase in 2015 because of rumors that if the two countries normalize relations, the United States would change immigration policies that allow Cubans who reach the United States to obtain status.

Central America

Weak institutions, poor economic prospects, and the growing strength of criminal gangs will probably limit the ability of the governments of Central America's northern tier—El Salvador, Guatemala, and Honduras—to improve rule of law, job opportunities, and citizen security, which will probably continue to fuel immigration to the United States in 2015. Fractured legislatures, political challenges, and entrenched business interests will probably slow agreement on raising some of the lowest tax collection rates in the world or adopting economic and social policies that would help reduce the high rates of poverty that spur migration to the United States. About 25 percent of **El Salvador's** population has emigrated during the past two decades, mostly to the United States, because of lack of economic opportunities and widespread insecurity. El Salvador's economy has experienced the lowest economic growth rates in the region for eight consecutive years. **Guatemala's** weak fiscal position will undermine efforts to ameliorate extreme poverty, particularly in rural areas. About 1.6 million Guatemalans reside in the United States and send about $5.5 billion in remittances back home each year. **Honduras**, one of the hemisphere's poorest countries, is struggling to make headway against ineffective, corrupt institutions. Honduras has the world's highest rate of homicides per capita, despite a reported modest decline in 2014, and criminal gangs are forcibly recruiting youth and extorting businesses and individuals.

Venezuela

Like most oil-exporting nations, Venezuela is experiencing the economic consequences of policy choices and the decline in global oil prices. Oil accounts for about 95 percent of Venezuelan export earnings and 45 percent of government revenue. Caracas will face a strained fiscal environment in 2015 along with rising inflation and shortages of essential goods.

24

Legislative elections are slated to occur by the end of 2015; voters will be concerned about public security, the economy, and political rights. President Nicolas Maduro appointed a presidential commission to review the country's police system and recommend reforms after the high-profile murder of a national assembly deputy and a violent law enforcement confrontation in October 2014 with a radical, armed group known as a *colectivo*.

Haiti

Political tensions between Haitian President Martelly and his opponents will probably flare during 2015 and might undermine preparations for overdue local and parliamentary elections as well as for the vote for a new president in November 2015. Haiti will need substantial technical and financial support from the international community to organize and hold elections. Some violent protests are probable and might become more intense or widespread if political opponents believe that electoral preparations favor Martelly's party or allies.